FRAMING NAGORNO-KARABAKH CONFLICT RESOLUTION: UNDERSTANDING THE REASONS FOR FAILURE AND ASSESSING THE FUTURE

More than 5000 days have passed since the signing of the May 1994 Russian-brokered cease-fire agreement that brought major combat operations to a halt in Nagorno-Karabakh. During this time, little has changed on the ground, with the opposing forces still occupying World War I style trenches on a 500-mile long line of contact.[1] While little has changed on the front lines in these 14 years, much has changed on the national-level political scene and security sector in Armenia, Azerbaijan and the Nagorno-Karabakh Republic. While these changes have had an increasingly negative impact on the possibility of conflict resolution, they also help to explain the underlying positions of the parties to the conflict and the reality of today's situation.

History also plays an important role in explaining why no resolution of this conflict has occurred to date. The history of the Armenian people is particularly critical to understanding why some of the above mentioned changes have taken place, why no resolution has occurred to date, and why the outlook for resolution will remain especially gloomy. The history of ethnic Armenians, that is to say, the populations of the Republic of Armenia proper and the so-called Nagorno-Karabakh Republic, is extremely relevant to any discussion of conflict resolution because the Armenian side was victorious in the conflict and therefore must now be convinced that returning to Azerbaijan the territory acquired during the conflict is in Armenia's long-term national interests.

---

[1] Neil Harvey, "Wires from the Front Line: Nagorno-Karabakh," BBC News, http://news.bbc.co.uk/1/hi/programmes/this_world/one_day_of_war/3622431.stm (accessed March 15, 2008).

1

The impact of Armenian history and the effects of recent political and security changes in the parties to the conflict clearly show why no resolution of the Nagorno-Karabakh conflict has been reached. For the same reasons, these factors show why conflict resolution will remain a near impossibility in the future, barring significant changes in the thinking of the leadership of the parties to the conflict. The dangerous rhetoric of the past few years only further complicates the chances for resolution, as it reduces confidence in the possibility of a peaceful approach and leads both sides to increase their preparation for renewed combat operations.

While many have pointed fingers at the OSCE, the European Union and the United Nations for their lack of effort or for their failure to adopt an effective approach to facilitating an end to the conflict, the reality of the situation is that resolution cannot be forced upon the parties to the conflict. The belief that Nagorno-Karabakh conflict resolution can be imposed upon the parties to the conflict by outside organizations reflects a lack of understanding of the true dynamics that have been determining the way ahead for this conflict and the region. Moreover, these same dynamics will continue to determine the way ahead for the region, leaving Nagorno-Karabakh conflict resolution an extremely remote proposition. Without conflict resolution, the prognosis for the future can include only two possible scenarios – a continuation of the standoff that has existed now for 14 years or renewed war.

Conflict in the Caucasus

The Caucasus has long been a crucible for conflict. For centuries it has served as a crossroads between East and West, between North and South, and between the Christian and Muslim worlds. This sub-region continues to serve today as a critical crossroads and still continues to provide a fertile environment for conflict. Of the 3000

kilometers (1860 miles) of international borders in the Caucasus today, only the nine-

kilometer (5.6 miles) stretch between Turkey and the Azerbaijani exclave province of

Nakhichevan can truly be called a friendly border.[2] Of the four protracted conflicts, or

so-called frozen conflicts, on the territory of the former Soviet Union, three are in the

South Caucasus. And while three of these conflicts are intrastate in nature[3], the Nagorno-

Karabakh conflict is considered to be interstate because it involves the nations of

Armenia and Azerbaijan, in addition to the so-called Nagorno-Karabakh Republic, a

breakaway republic of Azerbaijan whose territory is still recognized by international law

and the international community as part of Azerbaijan.

The Aftermath of War

     While each of these four protracted conflicts possesses its own complexities, the

Nagorno-Karabakh conflict presents a much more complex and difficult set of

circumstances for several reasons. The so-called Nagorno-Karabakh Republic, formerly

an autonomous region within the Soviet Union that was located within the borders of the

Azerbaijani Soviet Socialist Republic, declared its independence in a December 1991 by

a vote of its Supreme Soviet, a vote that passed overwhelmingly with the ethnic Azeri

members of the body abstaining.[4] The existence of this unrecognized, self-proclaimed

republic complicates the issue of conflict resolution because Nagorno-Karabakh officials

---

[2] "Where Worlds Collide," *The Economist*, August 19, 2000.
[3] The Transdniestria conflict is an intrastate conflict that pits this breakaway republic of Moldova against that Government. The conflicts in Abkhazia and South Ossetia, separate breakaway republics within Georgia, pit these republics against that nation.
[4] *Wikipedia*, s.v. "Nagorno-Karabakh," http://en.wikipedia.org/wiki/Nagorno-Karabakh (accessed March 14, 2008.

thrust themselves into pertinent issues and cause additional friction to that which already exists between Armenia and Azerbaijan.

At the signing of the cease-fire in May 1994, the Armenian side controlled a significant amount of territory recognized by international law and the international community as belonging to Azerbaijan. The Armenian side held, and still holds today, nearly all of the territory of the Soviet Union's Nagorno-Karabakh Autonomous Region, as well as most of the territory of the surrounding seven Azerbaijani provinces of Lachin, Kelbajar, Fizuli, Agdam, Jebrail, Zangelan and Kubatly.[5] A fair and detailed analysis of these territories under ethnic Armenian control shows them to be 13.62% of Azerbaijani territory.[6] Despite former Azerbaijani President Heydar Aliyev's 1993 statement that 20% of his country was occupied by the Armenians, and the repeating of that figure by his countrymen since then,[7] it appears that slightly less than 14% appears to be the most accurate assessment of the territory in question. This is nevertheless a significant percentage of territory, the loss of which is felt on a daily basis in Azerbaijan.

The changes in territorial holdings, not to mention the general effects of the war over Nagorno-Karabakh, created an enormous problem for the members of each ethnic group living as a minority among the other ethnic group. Ethnic Azeris were forced to leave Armenia proper and Nagorno-Karabakh, while ethnic Armenians were forced to leave Azerbaijan, creating staggering numbers of refugees and internally displaced persons. Approximately 353,000 Armenians fled Azerbaijan to Armenia and Russia, while about 750,000 Azerbaijanis fled Nagorno-Karabakh and the other territories for

---

[5] *Nagorno-Karabakh: Risking War*, International Crisis Group Europe Report Number 187, November 14, 2007, 1.
[6] Thomas de Waal, *Black Garden: Armenia and Azerbaijan Through Peace and War* (New York: New York University Press, 2003), 286.
[7] Ibid.

safer environs further east in Azerbaijan.[8] The burden on the Azerbaijani Government to find temporary shelter for such numbers of internally displaced persons in eastern Azerbaijan keeps this issue on the forefront of Azerbaijani discussions of the conflict.[9]

Another complicating factor of conflict resolution lies in the very status of Nagorno-Karabakh, which existed in the Soviet Union as the Nagorno-Karabakh Autonomous Region, but fell within the territory of the Soviet Socialist Republic of Azerbaijan. Armenian and Azerbaijani officials have different interpretations of Nagorno-Karabakh's status within the Soviet Union.

The Azerbaijani interpretation is that the territory of the Nagorno-Karabakh Autonomous Region of the Soviet Union was actually an integral part of the Azerbaijani Soviet Socialist Republic.[10] The Armenian position on the issue is that the territory of the Nagorno-Karabakh Autonomous Region was not an integral part of the territory of the Azerbaijani Soviet Socialist Republic, but was a truly autonomous region of the Soviet Union that was in no way officially linked to the Azerbaijani Soviet Socialist Republic.[11]

These respective positions on the territory of the Nagorno-Karabakh Autonomous Region as it existed under the Soviet Union are important because they explain the two nations' respective interpretations of this territory upon the dissolution of the Soviet Union. Azerbaijan views the territory in question as integral to the successor state of the Azerbaijani Soviet Socialist Republic, the Republic of Azerbaijan. Armenia, on the other

[8] Arif Yunusov, unpublished article "The Armenian-Azerbaijani Conflict: Aspects of Migration" in Zh. Zaionkovskaya (ed.) *The Migration Situation in CIS Countries* (in Russian), (Moscow, 1999).
[9] *Nagorno-Karabakh: Risking War*, International Crisis Group Europe Report Number 187, November 14, 2007, 11.
[10] Interview, politico-military analyst, Yerevan, July 1, 2007.
[11] Ibid.

hand, views this territory as an independent entity not integral to the Republic of Azerbaijan.

Despite its view on the status of Nagorno-Karabakh, the Government of Armenia has not officially recognized the independence of the self-proclaimed Nagorno-Karabakh Republic. In fact, no nation has recognized its independence. The Armenian Parliament has addressed this issue in 2007 and 2008, however, but ultimately decided to postpone a vote on recognizing the independence of the Nagorno-Karabakh Republic.[12]

Attempts at Conflict Resolution

While it is not important to determine where blame should lie for the lack of conflict resolution, it is important to examine the roles of entities and organizations involved in the diplomatic negotiations and processes that attempted to achieve this conflict resolution. Some analysts point to a lack of resolve on the parts of international or regional organizations as being significant factors contributing to the lack of resolution of the Nagorno-Karabakh conflict, such criticism really is misplaced.

The lead role in mediating a peaceful resolution of the Nagorno-Karabakh conflict fell to the so-called Minsk Group, a representative group of about a dozen participating states of the Organization for Security and Cooperation in Europe (OSCE) created in 1992 while combat operations were still ongoing in Nagorno-Karabakh.[13] The efforts of the Minsk Group to resolve the conflict have essentially been carried out through the

---

[12] GlobalSecurity.org, "Armenian Bill to Recognize Nagorno-Karabakh Criticized," http://www.globalsecurity.org/military/library/news/2007/08/mil-070828-rferl04.htm (accessed March 20, 2008).
[13] Organization for Security and Cooperation in Europe, "Minsk Process," http://www.osce.org/item/21979.html (accessed November 20, 2007).

group's three Co-Chairmen, senior diplomats from three Minsk Group countries, the U.S., Russia and France.

While the years immediately following the 1994 cease-fire showed the parties to the conflict not yet ready for serious discussion of conflict resolution, two significant spikes in Minsk Group Co-Chairmen efforts led Armenian and Azerbaijani officials to meet and seriously discuss the issues at hand, a promising sign to many that conflict resolution may have been likely. The first of these was a 2001 conference held in Key West that included representatives from Armenia, Azerbaijan and the three Co-Chair countries.[14] While this conference raised hopes of resolving the conflict, no agreement was reached and the details of the conference proceedings remained largely secret.[15]

The second spike in Minsk Group activity to resolve the conflict occurred over many months in 2006 and 2007, when significant Co-Chairmen engagement of Armenian and Azerbaijani officials resulted in several meetings of the two nations' presidents and foreign ministers.[16] These meetings led to the two parties' agreement on many principles of a potential peace deal, but three points proved too difficult for agreement and stalled further progress on the deal.[17] The specifics of this draft peace plan were not initially made public, but that changed in mid-2006, when the Co-Chairmen attempted to jumpstart the negotiation process by releasing the details of this developing framework

[14] Central Asia-Caucasus Institute, "Key West Talks on Nagorno-Karabakh: Will the Caucasian Knot be Cut," Johns Hopkins University, http://www.cacianalyst.org/?q=node/242 (accessed March 18, 2008).
[15] *Wikipedia*, s.v. "Nagorno-Karabakh Republic," http://en.wikipedia.org/wiki/Nagorno-Karabakh_Republic (accessed March 16, 2008).

[16] *Nagorno-Karabakh: Risking War*, International Crisis Group Europe Report Number 187, November 14, 2007, 1-3.
[17] Ibid, 2.

agreement between Armenia and Azerbaijan.[18] This release of information revealed the three sticking points of the draft deal – the withdrawal of forces, the status of a corridor in the Lachin province to provide passage between Armenia and Nagorno-Karabakh, and the nature and timing of a referendum vote on Nagorno-Karabakh's future status.[19]

Despite the lack of success in reaching a bona fide peace plan, the Minsk Group Co-Chairmen still pushed in 2007 for Armenia and Azerbaijan to sign a document of basic principles, which at least would codify the points on which the parties agreed and outline those still too problematic for agreement. Despite the significant effort to reach agreement on this front prior to major election cycles in both countries – the 2008 presidential election in Armenia and the 2009 presidential election in Azerbaijan – success proved elusive.

While criticism of United Nations efforts, or lack thereof, also has been voiced, the UN has not been completely idle. Four UN Security Council Resolutions were adopted during the war that call for the withdrawal of "local Armenian forces" from the territories of Azerbaijan, although this has not happened to date.[20] The conflict surfaced again in the UN in early 2008, when the UN General Assembly passed a nonbonding resolution introduced by Azerbaijan that demanded the "immediate, complete and unconditional" withdrawal of all Armenian forces from Azerbaijan's territory.[21] While this bill passed, with only 39 votes in favor and more than 100 abstentions, the three Minsk Group Co-Chair countries, the U.S. Russia and France, voted against the bill,

---

[18] Organization for Security and Cooperation in Europe, "Statement by the OSCE Minsk Group Co-Chairs," July 3, 2006, http://www.osce.org/item/19803.html (accessed November 20, 2007).
[19] *Nagorno-Karabakh: Risking War*, International Crisis Group Europe Report Number 187, November 14, 2007, 2.
[20] Ibid, 1.
[21] Today.AZ, "General Assembly of UN Adopts Resolution Reaffirming Territorial Integrity of Azerbaijan, Demanding Withdrawal of all Armenian Forces," http://www.today.az/news/politics/43734.html (accessed March 16, 2008).

which infuriated the Government of Azerbaijan to the point that it has begun examining procedures to withdraw from the Minsk Group process.[22] The mid-March 2008 introduction of this UN resolution by Azerbaijan is an additional counter-move to UN efforts in Kosovo that ultimately led to that province's declaration of independence in December 2007. On 4 March 2008, the Azerbaijani Parliament overwhelmingly approved President Ilham Aliyev's request to withdraw Azerbaijan's peacekeeping contingent from Kosovo.[23]

While none of these entities or organizations has had a perfect record, it must be said that, given the circumstances, the OSCE Minsk Group Co-Chairmen have done a solid job in facilitating the negotiation process between the parties to the conflict. Their efforts have ensured that some degree of continued interest in the negotiations process remains.

These organizations will only be successful to the degree that the parties to the conflict themselves show the willingness to make the necessary compromise that would allow the achievement of even some intermediate stage of resolution. For example, a recent call for the international community to impress on Armenia and Azerbaijan the need for progress in peace talks, as well as for European Neighborhood Policy funding to be linked to progress in negotiations[24] demonstrates the thinking that outside forces can impose conflict resolution on Armenia and Azerbaijan. This is, however, an approach that fails to recognize the depth of commitment each party to the conflict has to its cause.

---

[22] Radio Free Europe/Radio Liberty, "Azerbaijan Criticizes France, Russia, U.S. Over Karabakh Resolution," http://www.rferl.org/featuresarticle/2008/03/43a1d312-35e3-4cd7-b781-5542450988cf.html (accessed March 19, 2008).

[23] ReliefWeb, "Kosovo and Karabakh: How Azerbaijan Sees the Connection," http://www.reliefweb.int/rw/RWB.NSF/db900SID/SODA-7D94B2?OpenDocument (accessed March 30, 2008).

[24] Sabine Freizer, "Nagorno-Karabakh – A Frozen Conflict that Could Boil Over," International Crisis Group, http://www.crisisgroup.org/home/index.cfm?id=5277 (accessed February 10, 2008).

Both the UN and the OSCE do recognize that the international relations'

principles of self-determination and territorial integrity are both relevant to the discussion

of Nagorno-Karabakh conflict resolution,[25] a point that simultaneously recognizes the

major argument of each party as to why conflict resolution should proceed in accordance

with its desires. This allows both organizations to remain as neutral as possible in their

attempts to sort out the conflict.

The Benefits of Resolution

Western minds may find it natural to want to resolve the NK conflict, as

resolution would allow for the normalization of relations with neighbors, an improved

security situation, and the creation of the necessary conditions for broader and deeper

economic development in the entire region.

Western thinking can quickly grasp the overwhelming benefit that resolution of

the Nagorno-Karabakh conflict would bring not only to the belligerent parties, but also to

the entire region. With Armenian and Nagorno-Karabakh forces withdrawn from the line

of contact in Azerbaijani territory in accordance with the provisions of the peace deal,

Turkey and Armenia could move to address the reestablishment of diplomatic relations

and the opening of the Turkish-Armenian border that has been closed since 1993.[26] The

opening of this border would have significant impact on the Armenian economy – one

study estimated that a reopened Turkish-Armenian border would reduce transport costs

---

[25] Interview, senior Armenian diplomat, Vienna, January 14, 2008.
[26] de Waal, 277.

between the two countries by a third to a half, in turn increasing Armenia's GDP by 180 million dollars.[27]

Despite its borders with Azerbaijan being closed for 15 years, Armenia's economy has done surprisingly well. Annual GDP growth has been more than 13% over the past few years.[28] Granted, this growth is not occurring across the entirety of the Armenian economic spectrum – it is concentrated in a few sectors, namely construction and construction materials, precious and semi-precious stone refining and jewelry production.[29]

One could support an argument that the current Armenian leadership is in its initial stages of re-establishing some form of a Greater Armenia. The *de facto* situation in Nagorno-Karabakh and the other territories under Armenian control supports this argument. While the geopolitical landscape of the 21st century would make it extremely difficult for any additional expansion of this Greater Armenia, the territorial holdings acquired as a result of the Nagorno-Karabakh War are a significant victory, both an actual victory and a moral victory, for the ethnic Armenian side.

Azerbaijan and Turkey have adopted several fairly successful punitive steps against Armenia for its unwillingness to redeploy troops from internationally recognized Azerbaijani soil and return the Azerbaijani territories still being held illegally and in defiance of UN Security Council resolutions.

---

[27] Richard Beilock, "What is Wrong with Armenia?," Caucasus Regional Studies 4, 1(1999), http://www.ciaonet.org/olj/crs_1999/crs99_ber01.html (accessed March 31, 2008).
[28] *CIA World Factbook 2008*, s.v. "Armenia," https://www.cia.gov/library/publications/the-world-factbook/ (accessed April 17, 2008).
[29] Interview, politico-military analyst, Yerevan, July 1, 2007.

In addition to the closing of the borders, the path of the Baku-Tbilisi-Ceyhan (BTC) Pipeline, which transports Azerbaijan's Caspian oil to market via the Turkish Mediterranean port of Ceyhan, runs northwest through Azerbaijan, then purposely skirts Armenia to the north, running through Georgia then turning southwest to transit Turkey and reach the Mediterranean.[30] While the shortest distance between Baku and Ceyhan is directly through Armenia, no one should be surprised that Azerbaijan would not agree to the pipeline traversing the territory of a nation with whom such a dangerous ongoing conflict exists. While seen by Armenia as an additional provocative step to further isolate the country, Azerbaijan had little choice in protecting its interests in bringing its Caspian oil to the market.[31]

An additional issue that compounds Armenia's isolation is the creation of a new rail link between the northeastern Turkish city of Kars and the Georgian town of Akhalkalaki, a key rail segment that would complete the connection between Anatolian Turkey and Russia. This path for the rail link allows the route to bypass Armenia to the northwest, and was chosen for development despite an already existing rail link from the Turkish-Armenian border, just east of Kars, that runs through Armenia directly to Akhalkalaki.

The Important Effect of History

A senior diplomat from the Caucasus expressed the view that the U.S. and other nations are good at looking to the future to find what they perceive to be the proper path

---

[30] Institute for the Analysis of Global Security, "Baku-Tbilisi-Ceyhan Pipeline: Not Yet Finished and Already Threatened," http://www.iags.org/n1104041.htm (accessed March 20, 2008).

[31] Eurasia Daily Monitor, "Possible Rapprochement Between Armenia and Turkey," The Jamestown Foundation, http://www.jamestown.org/edm/article.php?article_id=2373047 (accessed April 2, 2008).

to conflict resolution, but are not as adept in looking to the past, to an appropriate degree, to understand the exact causes of conflict and how the ramifications of these causes still impact the current decision-making of the parties to the conflict.[32]

This is certainly true with respect to Nagorno-Karabakh resolution. Ironically, however, in this case it isn't necessarily the history of Nagorno-Karabakh itself that is influencing the Armenian leadership's stance on the conflict, but rather the broader and very sad history of the Armenian people. Several events in this history meld together to significantly influence the thinking of ethnic Armenians, in general, and specifically complicate the views of any potential Armenian leader, let alone one from Nagorno-Karabakh, with respect to foreign policy and with respect to resolution of the conflict.

The aspects of this sad history also help to explain why Armenian and Nagorno-Karabakh leaders have been and will remain extremely reluctant to return any territory gained in the region, let alone territory gained through the spilling of Armenian blood.

Throughout nearly the entirety of the history of the Armenian people, they have been on the losing end of conflicts. They have suffered at the hands of neighboring empires whose borders met and repeatedly changed in the South Caucasus. Other than a few brief episodes in history, they have always played the role of victim, suffering the consequences of the desires of Roman, Byzantine, Persian, Ottoman and Russian empires.[33] This fact is best evidenced by looking at Armenian independence over the past millennium, of which only two periods lasting a total of 18 years are on record. The first of these was from 1918 to 1920, when Armenia gained independence upon the dissolution of the Russian Empire at the end of the World War I, although was quickly

---

[32] Interview, senior Armenian diplomat, Vienna, 14 January 2008.
[33] Christopher J. Walker, *Armenia: The Survival of a Nation* (Chatham: Mckays, 1990), 25.

brought under Soviet control in 1920. Armenia's second period of independence is the current one, which has lasted 16 years, beginning with the nation's declaration of independence from the Soviet Union in September 1991.[34]

It is also a rather rare occurrence in Armenian history that the intermediate outcome of the Nagorno-Karabakh conflict, that is to say, the situation at the time of the 1994 cease-fire agreement signing, finds the Armenians victorious. This victory also provides an interesting irony – a role reversal has occurred for Armenia and it is filling the role of victor, not victim, while its opponent Azerbaijan is saddled with the victim complex.[35]

The current landmass of the Republic of Armenia is approximately 29,800 square kilometers, slightly smaller than the U.S. state of Maryland.[36] This puts Armenia at its smallest size in history and greatly pales in comparison to the territory of the Armenia Kingdom of the first century BC, often called the Three Seas Empire due to its east-west span stretching from the Black Sea to the Caspian Sea and its southernmost reaches touching the Mediterranean Sea.[37] Given the small amount of territory held by ethnic Armenians today, relative to their previous holdings, it is very understandable that ethnic Armenian leaders would hold at all costs any territory gained, whether the ultimate goal is creating a Greater Armenia or simply hedging against future loss of territory.

Another important aspect of Armenian history that bears on today's situation is one of the most notable milestones in that history, the acceptance of Christianity in 301 AD by Armenian King Tiridates (Trdat) and his decree that Christianity would be the

---

[34] *Wikipedia*, s.v. "Armenia," http://en.wikipedia.org/wiki/Armenia (accessed March 20, 2008).
[35] Interview, senior Armenian diplomat, Vienna, January 14, 2008.
[36] *CIA World Factbook 2008*, s.v. "Armenia," https://www.cia.gov/library/publications/the-world-factbook/ (accessed April 17, 2008).
[37] Armenia under Tigran the Great (map, in Armenian), Yerevan, 2003.

14

religion of his realm, thus making Armenia the first Christian nation.[38] This point cannot

be overlooked, as it helps to explain why the nation has had such a troubled past in this

very difficult region. In a region that is overwhelmingly Muslim, Armenia is a

significant exception with its remarkably homogeneous population that is more than 95%

ethnic Armenian and more than 95% Orthodox Christian.

The most tragic event in Armenian history, however, is the so-called Armenian

Genocide, where between 500,000 and 1.5 million Armenians suffered horrific deaths in

1915, the result of a campaign directed by the Ottoman leadership.[39] While many

European nations and 40 U.S. states have officially adopted resolutions condemning the

massacres of 1915 as genocide, Turkey sees these events as the unfortunate byproduct of

World War I combat operations between the Russian Empire and Ottoman Empire.[40]

These events of 1915 had such an enormously profound effect on surviving Armenians of

that era, and even on all ethnic Armenians today, that the collective Armenian psyche

cannot move beyond the issue.[41] In that respect, the 1915 genocide of the Armenians

mirrors the Holocaust's impact on the Jewish nation – it is the defining event of their

history that will never be forgotten, an event that galvanizes not only survivors, but also

future generations, and greatly impacts the political scene, most significantly in the

foreign policy arena.[42]

While many in the world are aware of this so-called Armenian Genocide of 1915,

because of the magnitude of this event, they are not aware of the broader scope of

---

[38] Walker, 24.

[39] *Wikipedia*, s.v. "Armenian Genocide," http://en.wikipedia.org/wiki/Armenian_Genocide (accessed May 19, 2008).

[40] *Wikipedia*, s.v. "Denial of the Armenian Genocide," http://en.wikipedia.org/wiki/Denial_of_the_Armenian_Genocide Genocide (accessed May 19, 2008).

[41] Interview, Yerevan State University professor, Yerevan, July 2, 2007.

[42] Interview, politico-military analyst, Yerevan, July 1, 2007.

pogroms against Armenians in the Ottoman Empire. These pogroms were not an ever-present phenomenon, but were episodic in nature between 1893 and 1923, and caused the deaths of several hundred thousand Armenians[43]. These additional tragedies can only reinforce the depth of Armenian feelings on this issue and the impact on their approach to regional issues.

Essentially, the early 1990s provided sad history of Armenians that allowed them very little independence. The Nagorno-Karabakh conflict galvanized the Armenian side; ethnic Armenians from Nagorno-Karabakh, Armenia proper and the Diaspora joined efforts to support the cause.[44] Another noteworthy point is that Armenians see the outcome of the Nagorno-Karabakh conflict as an example of Azerbaijan paying for the sins of its horrific treatment of ethnic Armenians in 1988 in the Azerbaijani cities of Baku and Sumgayit that was the genesis of the conflict in the first place in Armenian eyes.[45]

The fact that ethnic Azeris, the majority ethnic group in Azerbaijan, are a Turkic people also cannot be overlooked. Some Armenians even loosely call Azerbaijani citizens Turks. This ethnic link of Azerbaijan with Turkey, coupled with Turkey's very real support of Azerbaijan during and since the conflict, make the impact of the Armenian Genocide that much more relative to conflict resolution issues today.

Changes on the Political and Security Fronts

Major change has occurred in the Armenian political scene since the signing of the cease-fire in 1994. It has been significantly influenced by the Karabakh lobby, the

---

[43] *Wikipedia*, s.v. "Armenian Genocide," http://en.wikipedia.org/wiki/Armenian_Genocide (accessed May 18, 2008).
[44] Interview, senior Armenian diplomat, Vienna, January 14, 2008.
[45] Ibid.

most powerful hard-line force in Armenian politics today, which has been holding the posts of President, Prime Minister, Armed Forces Chief of Staff, and Chairman of the Parliamentary Standing Commission on Defense.[46] The hard-line positions of this lobby are reinforced in Parliament by two nationalist parties, the Republican Party and the Armenian Revolutionary Federation (Dashnaktstyun), which as of late 2007 respectively held 66 and 16 seats of the body's 131 seat total.[47] There are also an estimated 200,000-250,000 Armenians of Nagorno-Karabakh origin living in Armenia proper today,[48] which amounts to 6-8% of Armenia's population of approximately 3 million.[49]

This Karabakh influence has led to what can be called a Karabakhization of the Armenian leadership, a phenomenon that began in February 1997, when then-President of the Nagorno-Karabakh Republic, Robert Kocharian, thrust himself onto the Armenian political scene as the Prime Minister.[50] He then became Armenia's President in 1998, in an election that was marred by irregularities and violations according to international electoral observers.[51] Kocharian also won reelection in 2002 and served out his second five-year term, the maximum allowed by the Armenian Constitution. Kocharian's most significant political ally during these ten years was Serzh Sargsyan, former Deputy Minister of Defense of the Nagorno-Karabakh Republic, who during Kocharian's two terms as President of Armenia served as the nation's Minister of National Security, twice

[46] *Nagorno-Karabakh: Risking War*, International Crisis Group Europe Report Number 187, November 14, 2007, 17.
[47] Ibid.
[48] Ibid.
[49] *CIA World Factbook 2008*, s.v. "Armenia," https://www.cia.gov/library/publications/the-world-factbook/ (accessed April 17, 2008).
[50] *Wikipedia*, s.v. "Robert Kocharian," http://en.wikipedia.org/wiki/Robert_Kocharyan (accessed March 22, 2008).
[51] Ibid.

as its Minister of Defense, and from early 2007 as its Prime Minister.[52] Serzh Sargsyan continued his consolidation of power in Armenia during this time, receiving the ultimate benefit in February 2008 when he was declared the victor in Armenia's disputed Presidential election and succeeded Kocharian.[53]

The greater issue in this discussion is not the fact that Kocharian and Sargsyan simply came to Armenia from Nagorno-Karabakh, or even that they held top positions in the Nagorno-Karabakh Republic prior to their arrival onto the Armenian political landscape. The most compelling aspect of their previous lives in Nagorno-Karabakh is the significant roles they played in the Nagorno-Karabakh independence movement in the late 1980s and their roles during the war in the early nineties.[54]

Robert Kocharian was a founding member of the Nagorno-Karabakh independence movement and served as the Chief of the Defense Committee during the war in the early 1990s.[55] His success in those endeavors later propelled him to the Presidency of the Nagorno-Karabakh Republic.[56] Serzh Sargsyan was already a close associate of Kocharian, serving as the wartime de facto Deputy Minister of Defense of the Nagorno-Karabakh Republic during Kocharian's first years as president.[57]

An important glimpse into Sargsyan's feelings about the conflict and the desire to see it resolved can be seen in his unprompted comments at the close of a 2000 interview, remarking that "the most important thing is not the territory. It's that one ethnic group is

[52] *Wikipedia*, s.v. "Serzh Sargsyan," http://en.wikipedia.org/wiki/Serzh_Sargsyan (accessed April 22, 2008).
[53] Ibid.
[54] *Wikipedia*, s.v. "Robert Kocharian," http://en.wikipedia.org/wiki/Robert_Kocharyan (accessed March 22, 2008).
[55] *Nagorno-Karabakh: Risking War*, International Crisis Group Europe Report Number 187, November 14, 2007, 14.
[56] Ibid.
[57] Ibid.

left in Armenia. In Vardenis and other regions, the Azerbaijanis used to be 70% of the population. Our cultures are not compatible. We can live side by side, but not within each other….there are very few of us."[58]

The importance of Kocharian and Sargsyan serving as pivotal figures of Nagorno-Karabakh's independence movement and then as elder statesmen of the Nagorno-Karabakh Republic cannot be overstated. It is extremely doubtful that any official in today's Nagorno-Karabakh would not defer to their desires in determining the exact way ahead for resolution of the conflict. And that means deferring to their desires in determining the Republic of Armenia's actual position and negotiating position, determining the Nagorno-Karabakh Republic's actual position and negotiating position, and determining exactly what issues will be addressed in press releases, to include information, accurate or not, on the relationship between the Armenia and the Nagorno-Karabakh Republic or their respective positions on issues associated with the resolution of the conflict.

Not surprisingly, this Karabakhization of the Armenian leadership has been accompanied by a reciprocal Armenianization of Nagorno-Karabakh and the other seven Azerbaijani territories under Armenian control. One example of this Armenianization of Nagorno-Karabakh and the other territories is that the Armenian government provides aid and grants to these areas, almost as if they were bona fide districts of Armenia.[59] Additional proof of this Armenianization is seen in the fact that residents of these

---

[58] de Waal, 273.
[59] Interview, politico-military analyst, Yerevan, July 1, 2007.

territories are provided passports, visas and other consular services by the Armenian government.[60]

This evolving Armenianization of Nagorno-Karabakh and the surrounding territories can also be seen in the nature of maps currently being produced in Armenia. While many Armenian produced atlases and maps now depict Nagorno-Karabakh as an entity belonging to Armenia, still others depict Nagorno-Karabakh, as well as the additional Armenian held territories as integral to the Republic of Armenia.[61] In the simplest of analyses, these productions reflect the fact that Armenia won the war and all this territory in question. While cartographers don't determine policy, this phenomenon may be a significant contributing variable to the ease with which Armenian society could continue to accept an ever-increasing integration of these territories into the fabric of Armenian state structures.

The Ongoing Arms Race

Given the ultimate charge of national leaders to preserve the independence and security of their respective states, it follows that those with an increasing threat of armed conflict should prepare militarily as quickly and effectively as possible. Increased preparation by one side will lead to a counter move by the other side, however, and an arms race will begin, as is the case with Armenia and Azerbaijan.

Such arms races are accompanied by a parallel understanding of their inherent dangers however. Azerbaijan's 2007 National Security Concept itself states that "the excessive accumulation of armaments and weapons in the region undermines regional

---

[60] Ibid.
[61] World and Republic of Armenia Atlas (in Armenian) (Yerevan: MacMillan, 2003).

stability."[62] Nonetheless, any nation faced with a near term conflict will do all it can to ensure it is best prepared for that conflict.

While there was little change in both sides' holdings of major combat systems in the first ten years after the signing of the ceasefire, that began to change dramatically in 2004. On the verge of seeing significant profits from the Baku-Tbilisi-Ceyhan pipeline, Azerbaijan increased its defense expenditures by 51 per cent in 2004-2005, and another 82 per cent in 2006,[63] raising the nation's annual defense expenditures to just over $1 billion dollars, an amount equal to the entire national budget of Armenia.

The impressive ground systems acquired by Azerbaijan during this period include 105 T-72 main battle tanks, 12 Smerch multiple launch rocket systems, 72 MT-12 100mm anti-tank guns and 85 PM-38 120mm mortars.[64] As for Azerbaijani air force acquisitions, this period saw the inventory grow by six Su-25 ground attack aircraft and one Su-25UB fighter[65], complemented by the later acquisition of 14 MiG-29 fighters.[66] Azerbaijan also has improved the ability of its air force to conduct operations by modernizing seven military airfields.[67]

On the Armenia side, 15 Su-25 ground attack aircraft were purchased in 2004 and constitute nearly the entirety of the fixed wing combat aircraft of the Armenian Air Force. Armenia also has continued to reinforce its relationship with Russia, signing a 25-year basing agreement with Russia in 1997 that provides for the significant Russian

---

[62] National Security Concept of the Republic of Azerbaijan, 6.
[63] Stockholm International Peace Research Institute.
[64] Oleg Glashatov, "Azerbaijan Readies for a War with Karabakh. Would it Happen?," *Military Industrial Courier* (in Russian), UN Register of Conventional Arms, at http://disarmament.un.org./.
[65] Today.AZ, "Azerbaijan Shows MiG-29 Fighter Jets," http://www.today.az/news/politics/38475.html (accessed March 24, 2008).
[66] "Azerbaijan Air Force Confirmed as Recipient of MiG-29s as Economy, Defense Spending Grow", 3 April 2007, http:alanpetersnewsbriefs.blogspot.com/2007/04/defense-foreign-affairs-analysis.html.
[67] Glashatov.

military presence in Armenia, including 18 MiG-29 fighters in Yerevan, along with infantry, armor, artillery, air defense and other supporting regiments in Armenia's second largest city, Gyumri, on the Armenian-Turkish border.[68] Armenian and Russian air defense forces both possess the formidable S-300/SA-10 long range, medium-to-high altitude surface-to-air missile systems as a counter to threat aircraft.[69]

These acquisitions clearly communicate the understanding of both nations that renewed armed conflict is a very real possibility. In fact, the rhetoric of national leaders even reinforces the likelihood of renewed war. Azerbaijani President Ilham Aliyev has been quoted many times as saying that if the ethnic Armenian side did not withdraw its troops from the Azerbaijani territories and return this land, that Azerbaijan would take these provinces back through a military offensive.[70] While such statements are an understandable reflection of the frustration created by years of stalemate, they enflame an already tense relationship and cause additional wariness that is difficult to overcome.

The Big Picture: Russia and Turkey

It is often difficult enough to comprehend the motives and actions of Caucasus nations, but is that much more difficult to understand the picture when an additional layer of complexity is added to the picture in the form of Russian and Turkish influence.

It is impossible to know the exact depth to which Russia and Turkey sponsor Armenia and Azerbaijan, respectively, in the Nagorno-Karabakh conflict specifically and in their broader security interests in general. The degree to which Russia and Turkey

---

[68] *Wikipedia*, s.v. Russian 102nd Military Base, http://en.wikipedia.org/wiki/Russian_102nd_Military_Base (accessed March 28, 2008).
[69] *Wikipedia*, s.v. S-300, http://en.wikipedia.org/wiki/SA-10 (accessed March 28, 2008).
[70] Reuters, "Azerbaijan May Use Force in Karabakh After Kosovo," http://www.reuters.com/articleID=USL04930529 (accessed March 4, 2008).

respectively control the individual actions and negotiating positions of Armenia and Azerbaijan is debatable. Former Azerbaijani presidential aide Vafa Guluzade provided an interesting thought on the subject, stating:

> "When we say that the conflict into which we have been drawn is 'Armenian-Azerbaijani,' we mislead both others and ourselves. In reality, this is the latest action in the old Russian-Turkish confrontation, in which Armenia is only an executor of its master, but Azerbaijan is a little obstacle on this path to the main goal. It is known that even at the beginning of the century during the First World War, Russia used the Armenians against Turkey. History, apparently, is repeating itself."[71]

Russia and Turkey have a mutual concern with and distrust of one another that is underpinned by their common history – there are ten recorded so-called Russian-Turkish Wars, where the Russian Empire and Ottoman Empire fought for territory and influence along their shared border.[72] While these ten conflicts, not to mention the World War I operations pitting the two against one another, took place between empires no longer existing, today's Russian Federation and Turkey maintain the wariness of one another that has existed for several centuries. Though the Turkish-Soviet land border has been replaced by Turkish-Georgian and Turkish-Armenian land borders, the absence of a Turkish-Russian land border in the Caucasus does not decrease the nations concerns about their respective influence in the region.

The Future

Without resolution of the conflict, the prognosis for the future can include only two possible scenarios – a continuation of the standoff that has existed now for 14 years or renewed war. The bellicose rhetoric of the parties to the conflict paints a troubling

---

[71] *Zerkalo*, Baku, December 26, 1998.

[72] *Military-historical Dictionary*, s.v. Russian-Turkish War (in Russian), (Moscow, Russki Iazyk, 1999).

picture for the future, but also provides a glimpse into understanding the thinking and negotiating positions of the respective sides.

It is true that since the signing of the ceasefire, the respective leaderships of Armenia and Azerbaijan have believed that the side starting the next war in Nagorno-Karabakh would be the side that would lose that war, [73] but the big question is when the Azerbaijani view of this statement could change – when could Baku believe that a military offensive launched to regain its territory would have a good chance of succeeding? The stalemate of the past 14 years has existed because of the relative parity of weapons systems and a fairly stable balance of power. Can Azerbaijan's impressive acquisition of combat systems since 2004 change the leadership's view of this principal?

Critical to the outcome of the Nagorno-Karabakh fighting in the early 1990s is the fact that the ethnic Armenians there were fighting for their historical homeland and their existence, not some ideology. [74] This dynamic will hold true for the ethnic Armenian side for any future fighting in Nagorno-Karabakh. One significant unknown, however, is whether Azerbaijani Government could be successful in instilling this same dynamic in its own armed forces and citizenry alike, ideally creating an insurmountable will to retake the territory that even international law and the international community recognize as legally part of Azerbaijan. If such a will were developed, it could be a critical intangible to be considered in any analysis of the relative combat power of the two belligerent sides.

Even Turkey's former Air Force intelligence chief has stated that war is the only answer for Azerbaijan if it wants to retake Nagorno-Karabakh, further advising that

---

[73] Interview, senior Armenian diplomat, Vienna, January 14, 2008.
[74] Ibid.

Azerbaijan should improve its air defense capability and be prepared to conduct both air and land operations in order to be successful.[75]

There is a thin line between protracted conflict and the kind of intractable conflict that has developed in Palestine, Kashmir and the Basque region.[76] While the Nagorno-Karabakh conflict remains a protracted conflict, only the future will tell whether it becomes an intractable conflict.

While most analysts who study the region point to an Azerbaijani offensive to reclaim its lost territory as the most likely genesis of the next war, an unprovoked attack by the Nagorno-Karabakh Republic, in some kind of coordinated fashion with Armenia, cannot be ruled out. Even the former Defense Minister of the Nagorno-Karabakh Republic, Samvel Babayan, predicted that a significant Azerbaijani rearmament could push the Karabakh forces to launch a lightning attack to seize more territory, with the ultimate aim of forcing a total Azerbaijani capitulation.[77]

Much can also be learned from the recently completed national security documents of both countries. The 2007 National Security Strategy of the Republic of Armenia mentions Azerbaijan six times, proclaiming that "the key issue of the national security of the Republic of Armenia is the settlement of the Nagorno-Karabakh conflict."[78] This document also provides Armenia's view on why resolution of the Nagorno-Karabakh conflict is such a complex undertaking when it states in the section on use of force as an external threat to national security:

---

[75] Today.AZ, "Former Chief of Turkey's air force intelligence services: 'If Azerbaijan wants to own Karabakh, war is the only solution'," http://www.today.az/politics/43750.html (accessed March 15, 2008).
[76] Interview, senior Armenian diplomat, Vienna, January 14, 2008.
[77] de Waal, 279.
[78] "National Security Strategy of the Republic of Armenia", in *Armenian Army* (in English, Russian and Armenian), 2007, 106.

"The Republic of Azerbaijan continues to pursue an aggressive policy of militant posturing that explicitly threatens the national security of the Republic of Armenia and the Republic of Nagorno-Karabakh. Despite numerous factors preventing such development, openly militant statements articulated at the highest level cause to consider them as direct threats. In light of the heightened threat environment, there is an additional danger that the Republic of Turkey, a strategic partner of Azerbaijan, may pose an additional threat. Taking into consideration the universally known provisions of international law, the Republic of Armenia considers the trade and transport blockade imposed by Turkey and Azerbaijan as a use of force against the Republic of Armenia."[79]

In the May 2007 National Security Concept of the Republic of Azerbaijan, one quickly comprehends Azerbaijan's desire to clearly communicate that it is the aggrieved party – the document mentions Armenia 28 times, beginning in the introduction itself.[80] This document also notes that the Organization of Islamic Conference was the first organization to recognize and condemn Armenia as an aggressor in the Nagorno-Karabakh conflict.[81]

These national security documents show the two nations' overwhelming focus and concern with the conflict and each other. The public documents are even a significant vehicle to communicate one nation's thoughts on the conflict with the other nation and the rest of the world.

---

[79] Ibid.
[80] National Security Concept of the Republic of Azerbaijan, 11.
[81] Ibid.

Conclusion

Why have the parties to the Nagorno-Karabakh conflict not resolved it over the past 14 years? This is much more than a rhetorical question. It is, rather, a question whose multi-part answer clearly points to how remote the chances were for resolution during this period. More important, and more troubling, is the fact that future resolution of the conflict appears even more unlikely.

The spilled blood of the war and the continuing conflict remain a painful reminder of those events and the enemy responsible for them. The bad blood that has continued to grow because of the inherent distrust based on the conflict is also exacerbated by the region's history, the escalating arms race and bellicose rhetoric, and the influence of external actors, all of which complicate the picture even more.

Simply put, the parties to the conflict have not achieved resolution because there has been no real willingness to make the necessary commitment to the kind of fair compromise that resolution would require. Unfortunately, the current setting provides for many more questions than it does answers.

Although no mainstream Armenian political party maintains as part of its platform that Armenia will not return the seven Azerbaijani territories currently being held,[82] does it really make sense to do so? Why should the Armenian side return these territories they call a security belt because of the ideal buffer they form? Would the return of these territories be met with some reciprocal gain for the ethnic Armenian side in the form of major economic benefits or security guarantees that would far outweigh the advantage of holding on to these territories?

---

[82] Interview, senior Armenian diplomat, Vienna, 14 January 2008.

Why should the Azerbaijani side continue to tolerate a neighboring nation holding nearly 14% of its internationally recognized territory? Why shouldn't Azerbaijan continue to attempt to isolate Armenia in any way possible as a punitive measure that may ultimately force their neighbor to agree to a peace plan that includes the withdrawal of ethnic Armenian forces from the seven Azerbaijani territories surrounding Nagorno-Karabakh and the return of these territories to Azerbaijan?

These questions are much easier to pose than to attempt to answer. The answers to them will be known one day. Hopefully, these answers will be learned through the peaceful resolution of the conflict at some point in the future, rather than renewed war. Significant changes will have to occur in the thinking of the leadership of the parties to the conflict and the parties with significant interests in the region. For the foreseeable future, though, the state of Armenian-Azerbaijani relations will not allow for the kind of mutual trust and compromise required in order to resolve the Nagorno-Karabakh conflict. Sadly, the status quo appears to be the best hope.